Travel Guide

To Faro 2023

Embark on a Sensational Adventure:
Faro's Top Destinations Unveiled

Anthony L. Mark

Copyright © (2023) Anthony L. Mark

All rights reserved. No part of this book may be reproduced, stored in a retrieval system, or transmitted in any form or by any means, electronic, mechanical, photocopying, recording, or otherwise, without the prior written permission of the copyright owner, except for brief quotations embodied in critical reviews and certain other noncommercial uses permitted by copyright law.

Table Of Contents

INTRODUCTION
Welcome to Faro: A Brief Overview

GETTING TO KNOW FARO

PRACTICAL INFORMATION
Travelling to Faro
Getting Around the City
Accommodation Options
Currency and Banking

EXPLORING FARO'S OLD TOWN
Faro Cathedral: A Testament of Faith and Architecture
Arco da Vila: A Gateway to the Past
Museu Municipal de Faro: Uncovering Faro's Heritage
Exploring the Streets and Squares

ISLAND HOPPING IN RIA FORMOSA

Ria Formosa Natural Park: A Coastal Paradise

Ilha Deserta: The Deserted Island Retreat

Ilha da Culatra: A Fishing Community's Haven

Ilha da Faro: Sun, Sand, and Serenity

FARO'S CULTURAL HIGHLIGHTS

Faro Municipal Theater: A Stage for Art and Entertainment

Capela dos Ossos: The Chapel of Bones

Centro Cultural António Aleixo: Embracing Contemporary Art

Cultural Festivals and Events

GASTRONOMIC DELIGHTS OF FARO

Exploring Faro's Culinary Scene

Traditional Algarvian Dishes to Try

Seafood Extravaganza: Fresh Catches and

Delicacies

DAY TRIPS FROM FARO

Tavira: The Jewel of the Eastern Algarve

Lagos: Historic Port Town and Stunning Beaches

Silves: A Glimpse into the Algarve's Moorish Past

Sagres: Where Land Ends and Adventure Begins

OUTDOOR ADVENTURES IN FARO

SHOPPING AND SOUVENIRS

Traditional Crafts and Artisanal Products

Local Markets and Shopping Districts

Unique Souvenirs to Bring Home

PRACTICAL TIPS AND RESOURCES

Safety and Emergency Information

Useful Phrases and Language Tips

Recommended Websites and Apps

Additional Travel Resources

CONCLUSION

Reflecting on Your Faro Adventure

INTRODUCTION

Welcome to Faro: A Brief Overview

The Algarve region's main city of Faro in southern Portugal welcomes you with its illustrious past, priceless cultural riches, and mesmerising natural beauty.

Faro offers a wide range of attractions for every traveller, nestled amid the Atlantic Ocean's glistening seas and encompassing the breathtaking Ria Formosa Natural Park.

As you go through Faro, you'll see a city that skillfully combines elements of the past and the present. The Old Town, the city's historic core, is a labyrinth of winding cobblestone lanes, whitewashed homes, and quaint squares where historic sites mix with hip stores and bustling cafes.

Architectural marvels like the majestic Gothic Faro Cathedral and the mediaeval Arco da Vila, an entrance to the city's centre, serve as a platform for the city's history. The Faro Municipal Museum is home to an intriguing collection of items that shed light on the area's past.

Ria Formosa, which lies outside the city, appeals to its stunning natural scenery. An interconnected system of lagoons, marshes, and barrier islands make up this protected natural park. Discover the beautiful islands of Ilha Deserta, Ilha da Culatra, and Ilha de Faro where you will find pristine beaches, clear waters, and peaceful fishing villages.

A wide variety of artistic expressions are available in Faro's vibrant and diverse cultural landscape. While the Capela dos Ossos (Chapel of Bones) draws visitors with its morbid yet stupefying exhibitions, the Faro Municipal Theater presents engaging performances. Contemporary art exhibitions and cultural activities are included at the Centro Cultural António Aleixo, giving Faro's artistic landscape a contemporary edge.

The gourmet delights of Faro will satisfy food enthusiasts. Try some of the local specialties, like cataplana, shellfish, and hearty stews. Enjoy some of the region's well-known sweets, including Dom Rodrigo and pastéis de nata. Don't forget to have a glass of regional wine or a drink of medronho, a traditional liquor created from arbutus tree fruit.

Everyone can find something to do in Faro, whether they like to spend their time exploring the outdoors through activities like birdwatching, hiking, or water sports.

This travel manual will take you on a journey across Faro, revealing its secret attractions, useful advice, and amazing encounters.

Prepare to enjoy the city's enchantment and set out on a thrilling journey unlike any other. Greetings from Faro!

GETTING TO KNOW FARO

1. Faro, the regional capital of southern Portugal's Algarve, is situated on the easternmost point of the Algarve coast. The picturesque Ria Formosa, a protected natural park famous for its lagoons, islands, and varied ecosystems, borders the city, which is situated along the Atlantic Ocean.

   Due to its distinctive combination of coastal beauty and enthralling scenery, Faro is a well-liked vacation spot for nature lovers.

2. Faro experiences a Mediterranean climate with long, hot summers and mild winters. The city experiences plenty of sunshine all year long, with summertime highs frequently topping 30°C (86°F). The seasons of spring and autumn are pleasant, while the winters

are still mild by European standards. Faro is a desirable travel destination all year round due to the pleasant weather and plenty of sunshine.

3. Faro has a long history with a deep cultural significance that goes back thousands of years. Initially built by the Romans, the city was later inhabited by the Moors during their dominance over the Iberian Peninsula.

   Faro has experienced several historical occurrences, such as the Portuguese reconquest in the 13th century and the disastrous earthquake of 1755, which had a profound effect on the city's urban planning and architecture.

4. The Old Town of Faro, which has been well-preserved, is where visitors may experience a sense of time travel thanks to its winding lanes, traditional

homes, and historical sites. Faro Cathedral, a spectacular Gothic building that displays the impact of several architectural styles over the ages, is located in the city's historic district. The city's historic walls and the mediaeval Arco da Vila doorway stand as reminders of Faro's past.

5. **Local Customs and Etiquette:** To ensure a polite and enjoyable stay in Faro, it is helpful to be knowledgeable of the local customs and etiquette. The majority of Portuguese people, especially those in Faro, are cordial, hospitable, and welcoming.

In Faro, there are a few customs and etiquette rules that are followed:

- It is traditional to shake hands and make direct eye contact when greeting someone. When entering stores, dining establishments, or conversing with locals, it is customary to say "Bom dia" (Good morning), "Boa tarde," or "Boa noite."

- **Politeness**: When addressing someone they don't know well, Portuguese people frequently use titles like "Senhor" (Mr.) or "Senhora" (Mrs./Ms.). It is considered courteous to say "Por favor" (Please) and "Obrigado/a" (Thank you).

- **Punctuality**: In Faro, being on time is generally praised. To avoid missing appointments, meetings, or tours, be on time.

- The mood of Faro is laid-back and easygoing, especially in the summer. However, it is advised to wear modestly and politely when attending places of worship or formal settings, covering shoulders and knees.

In Faro, tipping is customary at eateries, cafes, and pubs. The standard gratuity is 10%, but rounding up the total is also appropriate. It is normal to round up the fare in cabs.

By keeping in mind these traditions and manners, you may respect the Faro locals, participate in the local culture, and establish a good rapport with them while you are there.

PRACTICAL INFORMATION

Travelling to Faro

As a well-liked tourist location, Faro is well-connected and simple to get to using many modes of transportation. There are several alternatives to think about while organising your trip to Faro, whether you're travelling from inside Portugal or from outside.

1. **By Air:** Just a few miles west of the city's core lies Faro International Airport (FAO), which provides service to Faro. The airport offers flights by both domestic and foreign airlines and has excellent connections to key cities throughout Europe.

    Direct flights are available from several European locations, including well-known hubs like London, Dublin,

Amsterdam, Madrid, and Frankfurt, to Faro. You can take a cab, bus, or rental car from the airport to get to the city centre. All three options are widely available there.

2. **By Train**: Faro may be reached by train through the Portuguese railway network known as CP (Comboios de Portugal). Regular trains connect Faro to several Portuguese cities, such as Lisbon, Porto, and other communities along the Algarve coast.

   Train rides are relaxing and beautiful, letting you take in the beautiful scenery as you move. The Faro train station is conveniently situated in the middle of the city, making it simple to go to adjacent lodging and attractions.

3. **By Bus**: Faro has a robust bus network that connects the city to several

domestic and foreign locations. A hub for both local and long-distance buses, the bus station is close to the city's core. For visitors visiting the Algarve or coming from other regions of Portugal and Spain, numerous bus companies run routes to and from Faro, offering easy travel options.

4. **By Car:** Renting a car is a popular choice in Faro if you like the convenience and independence of travelling by automobile. Through a system of highways and major roads, the city is well-connected to the rest of Portugal.

Along the Algarve coast, the A22 highway—also known as the Via do Infante—provides access to Faro from both the west and the east. You have the freedom to see Faro and its surroundings at your speed when you rent a car.

5. Within the City: Navigating Faro is not too difficult once you get there. The city core is small and easily walked around. Additionally, Faro boasts a trustworthy public transportation network that includes buses that service a variety of communities and tourist destinations.

Taxis are frequently available and can be found at marked taxi stands or flagged down on the street. In Faro, cycling is also becoming more and more popular, and you may rent bikes to explore the city and its surroundings.

Think about the best form of transportation for your journey to Faro based on your preferences, spending limit, and itinerary.

Reaching Faro is a simple and convenient journey whether you decide to fly, ride a train, bus, or drive, setting the stage for a wonderful adventure in this enchanting city.

Getting Around the City

Due to its small size and well-established transportation system, Faro provides several practical options for moving around the city. There are options to fit your preferences and aid in your exploration of all that Faro has to offer, whether you choose to walk, take the bus, or rent a car.

1. **Walking**: It is simple to navigate the city core of Faro on foot, especially its lovely Old Town. Historic sites, pedestrian-only zones, and the city's winding lanes are all close by. You may immerse yourself in the city's ambiance

while strolling through it, find undiscovered areas, and take your time to admire the architecture.

2. **Public transit**: Faro offers an efficient and reasonably priced bus-based public transit system. The bus network connects the city's neighbourhoods, points of interest, and adjacent locations throughout the entire city and its outskirts.

   Tickets for buses can be bought from the driver or at specific ticket offices, and prices are typically affordable. It is simple to organise your trips thanks to the availability of timetables and route maps online and at bus stops.

3. **Taxis**: If you're travelling with a lot of luggage or have restricted mobility, taking a taxi is a practical way to navigate around Faro. Taxis can be

located at designated taxi stands, hailed on the street, or reserved via phone apps. The approximate fee should be confirmed with the driver before beginning your trip because fare rates are metered and regulated.

4. **Bicycles**: Faro provides bike-friendly infrastructure and rental services as cycling becomes more and more popular there.

You may cover more land while taking in the beautiful pathways and the city's coastline charm by touring Faro on a bicycle. In the city centre and close to famous tourist destinations, you may find bike rental shops that offer a variety of bicycles to fit your interests.

5. **Car rental**: If owning your vehicle gives you more freedom and flexibility, Faro offers car rental services. By renting a

car, you may travel at your own pace both within the city and around the greater Algarve region. It should be noted that parking in the city centre might be scarce, particularly during the busiest travel times, therefore it is wise to confirm parking policies and options before leaving.

It's crucial to take into account the unique requirements of your trip and select the most appropriate method of transportation in accordance. You can easily travel to Faro and make the most of your time seeing its historical landmarks, coastal scenery, and cultural treasures thanks to the city's small size and wealth of possibilities.

Accommodation Options

A variety of lodging choices are available in Faro to accommodate various tastes, financial constraints, and travel preferences. There are many lodging options in Faro, whether you're looking for opulent hotels, affordable hostels, or welcoming guesthouses, to ensure a comfortable stay while you're there. Here are a few well-liked lodging choices:

1. **Hotels**: Faro has a variety of lodging options to suit all tastes and price ranges. There are many options to pick from, ranging from opulent 5-star hotels with first-rate amenities and beautiful vistas to mid-range hotels that offer cosy rooms and practical conveniences.

   To make your stay more enjoyable, many hotels in Faro provide extras like swimming pools, exercise facilities, on-site restaurants, and concierge services.

2. **Guesthouses and Bed & Breakfasts:** Opt for a guesthouse or bed & breakfast (B&B) for a more individualised and private experience. These lodgings frequently have a homey, pleasant feel and are owned by families.

   Guesthouses and B&Bs offer cosy accommodations, hearty breakfasts, and attentive service. They offer a warm and genuine experience, whether they are found in the heart of the city or on its outskirts.

3. **Hostels**: If you're on a tight budget or prefer a more sociable setting, hostels are a terrific choice. Numerous hostels in Faro provide private rooms with common bathrooms and

dormitory-style lodging. Common amenities including kitchens, living rooms, and outdoor areas are frequently offered by hostels so that guests can mingle. Backpackers, lone travellers, and anyone looking for an exciting and economical lodging experience frequently choose them.

4. Apartments and vacation rentals are the best options for visitors who want more solitude and independence during their time in Faro. There are several short-term rental apartments and homes that offer completely equipped rooms, kitchens, and occasionally other amenities like swimming pools or access to private beaches.

There are several places where you may find vacation rentals, so you can pick one that best meets your interests.

5. **Camping**: For those who enjoy the outdoors and the outdoors, Faro provides camping choices that let you take in the natural beauty of the area. There are campgrounds with amenities for tents and campervans close to the city or in the surrounding areas.

   Camping offers chances for outdoor pursuits like hiking and beach exploration and is a cost-effective way to see Faro's scenery.

When selecting your lodging, keep things like location, accessibility to transit and attractions, amenities provided, and price range in mind. It is advisable to reserve your lodging in advance, especially during the busiest travel times, to ensure that you get your first option.

You can discover the ideal location to unwind and recharge during your visit thanks to the wide variety of lodging choices available in Faro.

Currency and Banking

1. **Currency**: The Euro (€) is Portugal's official unit of exchange. The Euro is recognized as a legal tender in Faro because it is a part of Portugal. It's a good idea to carry some Euros with you in case you need to pay for modest expenses like small purchases or public transit fares.

2. **Currency Exchange:** The Faro Airport, banks, exchange offices, and a few hotels offer currency exchange services. Banks normally provide cheap

exchange rates but can have sporadic hours of operation. Another choice is exchange bureaus, which are frequently found in tourist regions but their prices can differ. To get the greatest deal, it is advisable to compare rates and fees before exchanging your currency.

3. **ATMs**: Multibancos, often known as ATMs or Automatic Teller Machines in Portugal, are extensively available in Faro. They are everywhere in the city, including banks and commercial malls.

   You can use your debit or credit card at ATMs to get cash in euros. It is useful for foreign travellers as they typically provide instructions in a variety of languages. It's a good idea to check with your bank in advance because you should be aware that your bank can impose foreign transaction fees for ATM withdrawals.

4. **Credit Cards:** The majority of hotels, restaurants, stores, and tourist attractions in Faro accept credit cards, mainly Visa and Mastercard. For smaller stores or in case you run into places that don't accept cards, it's best to have some cash on hand. To prevent any potential problems with card usage when using your credit card, it's a good idea to let your bank know in advance about your vacation plans.

5. **Banking Hours**: Banks in Faro often have various hours from Monday through Friday. The regular business hours for banks are 8:30 AM to 3 PM. Some major banks might have extended hours or have locations in malls with extended hours, including Saturdays. To make sure they are open

when you need their services, it is advised to check the exact operation hours of your bank or the bank you wish to visit.

Money Exchange Advice:

- If you want to have some cash on hand for immediate costs when you arrive in Faro, think about exchanging a modest amount of money.

- Use ATMs to withdraw money because they frequently offer fair exchange rates. However, pay attention to any fees your bank may impose.

- Inform your bank of your travel intentions and ask whether there are any foreign transaction fees or ATM withdrawal restrictions.

- When using ATMs or exchanging money in public places, be vigilant and watch your things at all times.

You may efficiently manage your funds throughout your time in Faro and enjoy a smooth and hassle-free experience by being prepared with the local currency and being aware of the various banking choices.

EXPLORING FARO'S OLD TOWN

Faro Cathedral: A Testament of Faith and Architecture

In the middle of the city's historic district, the Faro Cathedral, also known as Sé de Faro, stands as a tribute to both religion and architectural genius.

This remarkable building has a key role in Faro's cultural heritage because of its exquisite details and lengthy history. Here is a deeper look at Faro Cathedral and some of its unique characteristics:

1. **History**: The Faro Cathedral was built in the 13th century, following the Christian reconquest of the area, on the site of a mediaeval mosque. The cathedral underwent numerous

architectural alterations and additions over the years, culminating in its distinctive fusion of Gothic, Renaissance, and Baroque styles.

2. **Exterior**: Faro Cathedral's exterior is breathtaking. With influences from the Manueline architecture style, which is distinguished by maritime motifs and decorative embellishments, its magnificent entrance displays complex masonry and sculptural details.

The bell tower of the cathedral, which is 30 metres (98 feet) tall, serves as a conspicuous landmark on the city's skyline.

3. **Interior**: Enter Faro Cathedral to view the stunning interior. With its towering pillars and arches, the main nave exudes grandeur and openness. Admire the exquisitely painted oak ceiling that

is covered with complex themes and patterns by looking up. Each chapel in the cathedral has a distinctive design and is home to religious altarpieces and works of art that add to the overall beauty.

4. **Museum and Rooftop Views**: The cathedral complex has a museum where a variety of religious objects are on show. These include statues, paintings, and ceremonial clothing.

The history and artistic legacy of the cathedral and the surrounding area can be explored in further detail by visitors. Furthermore, reaching the cathedral's rooftop terrace will reward you with spectacular perspectives of the city's rooftops and the surrounding area for those seeking panoramic views of Faro.

5. Faro Cathedral continues to be a busy site of worship, conducting religious services and festivals. It plays a significant part in the citizens of the city's spiritual lives and houses the Faro Bishop.

You can appreciate the Faro Cathedral's architectural beauty, religious fervour, and historical significance by paying a visit. If you're interested in the city's cultural riches, Faro Cathedral is a must-see location. Its external details, interior splendour, or fascinating history will all captivate you.

Arco da Vila: A Gateway to the Past

The majestic doorway that leads visitors into Faro's illustrious history is the Arco da Vila, which is located in the centre of the city's historic district. This mediaeval arch invites you to explore the charming streets and fully immerse yourself in the Old Town's allure as a symbol of Faro's history and cultural heritage. Let's examine the significance of the Arco da Vila in more detail:

1. **Historical Significance:** The Arco da Vila, often referred to as the Arch of the Town, has served as a significant entryway to the walled city of Faro for many years. Although the arch's origins go considerably further back in time—possibly all the way to the Roman era—it was built in the 19th century.

   It served as a fortified entrance gate, permitting access to the city while guarding it from dangers from without. Arco da Vila evolved into a representation of Faro's past and a link to it over time.

2. **Architectural Features**: Arco da Vila's architecture is an intriguing synthesis of various styles. The archway displays a variety of styles, including aspects from the Renaissance, Gothic, and Moorish periods.

   You'll notice beautiful masonry, colourful carvings, and delicate details as you go closer to the arch, all of which showcase the time's artistry. A clock tower perched above the arch gives the building more charm and improves its aesthetic appeal.

3. **Entrance to the Old Town**: Entering Arco da Vila is like going back in time. After passing through the arch, you'll be on Rua da Cidade, a charming street surrounded with old buildings, hospitable cafes, and conventional stores. This busy street goes farther into the Old Town, where you may

meander through tiny cobblestone alleyways, discover secret plazas, and come across historical sites.

4. Arco da Vila is a representation of Faro's cultural heritage and acts as a symbol of the city's history. Because of its magnificence and historical significance, it has become a recognizable landmark in Faro that appeals to both tourists and locals. The arch serves as a link between the contemporary city and the extensive historical fabric that is included within its boundaries.

5. Arco da Vila makes for a beautiful backdrop for photography, letting you capture the spirit of Faro's history and architectural grandeur. An eye-catching sight that perfectly captures the charm of the Old Town is created by the arch's detailed detailing,

brilliant colours, and beautiful proportions.

Arco da Vila offers a look into Faro's fascinating past and welcomes you to start an exploration adventure through the city's old quarter. Prepare to be transported to a bygone period as you travel under this magnificent arch and learn about the riches that are waiting for you in Faro's picturesque street and lanes.

Museu Municipal de Faro: Uncovering Faro's Heritage

Visitors may explore Faro's rich past and learn about its intriguing history at the Museu Municipal de Faro, a mesmerising facility that is situated in the centre of the city. The museum, which is housed in a former convent, has an extensive collection of relics, works of art, and exhibitions that give details about the area's cultural, archaeological, and aesthetic features. What to expect when visiting the Faro Municipal Museum is as follows:

1. **Exhibits and Collections:** The museum's exhibits are made to highlight the history of Faro, which spans from antiquity to the present. Archaeological relics, historical artefacts, religious artwork, sculptures, paintings, and decorative arts are all included in the collection.

   You will get the chance to learn about several eras and facets of Faro's past, including the Roman occupation, the influence of the Moors, and the city's function as a thriving maritime centre.

2. The museum's archaeology department contains a wide variety of objects that

illustrate Faro's earliest history. These relics, which range from Roman pottery and coinage to Moorish ceramics and Islamic ornamental items, provide a window into the lives and cultures of earlier civilizations. The exhibits offer insightful historical context and emphasise the importance of Faro as a significant cultural crossroads throughout history.

3. **Religious Art and Sculptures:** The museum's collection of religious artwork and sculptures serves to highlight Faro's rich religious past. These pieces of art span the mediaeval, Renaissance, and Baroque eras, representing a variety of styles and periods.

Admire ornately carved wooden sculptures, painted panels, sacred relics, and clothing used in religion, which let you comprehend the city's spiritual traditions better.

4. **Temporary Exhibitions**: The Municipal Museum of Faro frequently presents transient exhibitions that concentrate on particular subjects, creators, or historical eras. By presenting modern artwork, photography, or creative retellings of the city's past, these exhibits provide a new angle on Faro's background.

To find out what temporary exhibits are on show while you are there, see the museum's calendar.

5. **Convent Setting**: The museum's old convent setting contributes to its distinctive atmosphere. You may enjoy the tranquillity and architectural splendour of the monastery as you stroll around the hallways and galleries,

taking in the cloisters, arches, and quiet courtyards. By fostering a peaceful atmosphere for exploration and reflection, this setting improves the whole museum experience.

6. **Educational Programs and Events:** Throughout the year, the Municipal Museum of Faro also puts on educational programs, workshops, and cultural gatherings. These events give visitors of all ages the chance to interact with the museum's exhibits, discover Faro's history, and take part in practical activities.

A trip through the city's past and a fuller appreciation of its cultural significance may be found at the Museu Municipal de Faro. The museum's exhibits and artefacts will envelop you in the rich tapestry of Faro's legacy, whether you are interested in archaeology, art, or the history of the area.

Exploring the Streets and Squares

Getting lost in Faro's historic centre's winding alleyways and attractive squares is one of the pleasures of travelling there. The Old Town is a pedestrian-friendly region where you are encouraged to explore at your speed, finding hidden jewels and absorbing the lively ambiance. The following Faro streets and squares are worth exploring:

1. One of the principal streets in the Old Town is Rua de Santo António, where you should begin your excursion. This bustling street is studded with stores, cafes, and eateries that provide a variety of regional goods, trinkets, and culinary treats. Enjoy the lively atmosphere, look through the shops, and pause for a cup of coffee or a mouthwatering pastry.

2. Continue your stroll along the lovely street famed for its traditional homes

and vibrant façade, Rua Dom Francisco Gomes. You can find charming boutiques, art galleries, and little artisan stores here that sell one-of-a-kind handmade goods and regional artwork. It's a terrific spot to find genuine presents and souvenirs.

3. **Largo da Sé:** The square in front of Faro Cathedral, Largo da Sé, serves as a hub for activity in the Old Town. Orange trees, a lovely fountain, and outdoor cafes surround this charming square. Sit down, unwind, and enjoy the historical surroundings for a moment. You may take in views of the cathedral's stunning front and take in the bustling street life from here.

4. **Largo do Carmo**: Another gorgeous Faro square that is worth your attention is Largo do Carmo. The Igreja do Carmo, a charming church with a

distinctive tiled front, is located there. The square frequently hums with activity, hosting local events, musicians, and street performers. Take a seat at a cafe outside and take in the bustling scene.

5. **Largo de San Francisco:** Visit Largo de San Francisco, a charming square brimming with personality and history. This square has a lovely statue of St. Francis and is flanked by old houses. It's a calm place to unwind and observe the surroundings. From here, you can carry on your investigation by meandering into the neighbouring neighbourhoods, where you'll discover additional undiscovered treasures.

6. Praça Ferreira de Almeida is a bustling square close to the marina and is often referred to as Praça da Restauraço. Particularly in the evenings when locals

and tourists congregate to take in the bustling atmosphere, this area is a hive of activity. There are lots of eateries, cafes, and bars where you may enjoy delectable food and take in Faro's nightlife.

7. **Rua Vasco do Gama:** Visit Rua Vasco da Gama for a taste of regional cuisine. Traditional pubs and eateries serving Algarvian delicacies can be found on this street. Enjoy fresh seafood dishes, the traditional seafood stew cataplana, or other local specialties. The street offers a vibrant gastronomic experience and is frequently packed with residents.

Be sure to embrace the spirit of exploration as you stroll through the old district of Faro and permit yourself to become lost in its picturesque lanes and secret spaces. The Old Town is full of surprises, and each street and plaza has its special charm, giving you a lasting impression of the lively atmosphere and extensive history of the city.

ISLAND HOPPING IN RIA FORMOSA

Ria Formosa Natural Park: A Coastal Paradise

The Ria Formosa Natural Park, which is located near Faro, is a spectacular coastal paradise that mesmerises tourists with its pristine landscapes, varied ecosystems, and breathtaking beauty.

This protected area, which spans more than 18,000 hectares, has a network of lagoons, marshes, dunes, and barrier islands. What to expect when visiting the Ria Formosa Natural Park is as follows:

1. Several barrier islands, each with its appeal, may be found in the Ria Formosa Natural Park. Barreta Island, sometimes called Ilha Deserta, is a

tranquil uninhabited island famed for its immaculate white sand beaches and blue waters. Ilha da Culatra is a bustling fishing village with brightly painted homes, picturesque streets, and stunning beaches. The island of Ilha de Faro, which is in front of the city, combines urban conveniences with natural splendour.

2. **Beaches**: Ria Formosa is home to some stunning beaches. They are a sanctuary for beach lovers with their golden sands and clear waters.

   The natural park offers a variety of beach options for any preference, whether you choose to unwind on the isolated stretches of Ilha Deserta, soak up the sun on the long, sandy beaches of Ilha da Culatra, or take advantage of the family-friendly ambiance on Ilha da Faro.

3. Ria Formosa is a haven for those who love the natural world, especially birdwatchers. The park is the perfect place to go birdwatching because it serves as an important stopover for migratory birds.

   Ria Formosa offers numerous opportunities to see these avian marvels in their natural habitat because of its more than 200 bird species, which include flamingos, spoonbills, and other waders. Other animals that live in the park include chameleons, seahorses, and several fish species.

4. **Trails for walking and bicycling**: Ria Formosa has a vast network of trails for walking and bicycling that let tourists experience its many different landscapes. Wander through the salt marshes on the elevated wooden walks,

which offer sweeping views of the surrounding landscape and the lagoons. Additionally, there are bike lanes that you may use to explore the park's secret areas and immerse yourself in its serenity.

5. **Kayaking and Boat Tours:** Take a kayaking trip or join a boat excursion to discover Ria Formosa's waterways. Many travel companies provide escorted boat tours that take you through the waterways, islands, and marshes.

These excursions offer chances to see wildlife, discover the ecosystem of the park, and take in the stunning view from a new angle. Another well-liked method for exploring the park's tranquil waters and learning about its isolated coves is kayaking.

6. Visit one of the park's visitor centres to learn more about Ria Formosa's natural and cultural history. Environmental education. These facilities provide instructive exhibits, engaging displays, and instructional materials that highlight the ecosystems of the park, conservation activities, and regional customs.

   They improve knowledge of the park's value and promote environmental consciousness.

The Ria Formosa Natural Park offers an unrivalled coastal paradise to explore, whether you're looking to unwind on beautiful beaches, go birdwatching, or have an immersive nature experience. Experience the stunning scenery, rare animals, and solitude of this extraordinary natural jewel close to Faro.

Ilha Deserta: The Deserted Island Retreat

Barreta Island, also known as Ilha Deserta, is a hidden jewel in the Ria Formosa Natural Park that provides a genuinely exceptional and serene escape for nature enthusiasts and people looking for a peaceful beach experience. The following are some reasons to visit Ilha Deserta:

1. **Pristine Beaches**: Ilha Deserta is well known for its pristine, undeveloped beaches, which are frequently ranked among the most stunning in the Algarve. A picture-perfect paradise is created by the island's extensive stretches of smooth, white sand and the blue waters surrounding it.

   The serene beaches of Ilha Deserta offer a tranquil retreat from the busy mainland, whether you're wanting to laze in the sun, stroll along the shore, or take a cooling swim in the water.

2. **Peace & Seclusion:** Ilha Deserta is an uninhabited island free of development and mass tourism, living up to its name. It's quiet surroundings and a small population of visitors foster a sense of calm and privacy.

   You can locate a quiet area where you can relax, take in the sounds of nature, and experience the pleasure of having a beautiful beach almost entirely to yourself. It's the ideal getaway for anyone looking for a serene setting surrounded by untainted nature.

3. Ilha Deserta is a haven for lovers of the natural world and wildlife. The Ria Formosa Natural Park, which is home to a wide variety of bird species and other wildlife, includes the island.

Watch for flamingos, herons, sandpipers, and other bird species that live in the marshes and lagoons as you explore the island. Ilha Deserta's pristine setting offers a special chance to get in touch with nature and take in the splendour of its ecosystems.

4. **Nature Walks and Hiking**: While on Ilha Deserta, make use of the hiking and nature trails the island has to offer. Take a stroll among the dunes, marshes, and salt pans along the routes that have been set aside so you can take in the natural beauty of the island.

These strolls give you a chance to get up close and personal with the indigenous flora and fauna while taking in the tranquil atmosphere of the island.

5. Ilha Deserta is well-known for its excellent fish, another culinary delight. Visit Estaminé, the only restaurant on the island, which is renowned for its delectable and fresh fish dishes. Enjoy delectable seafood specialties while taking in panoramic views of the natural world. Savour the tastes of the Algarve's coastal cuisine.

6. **Boat Trips & Access**: Getting to Ilha Deserta from Faro involves a beautiful boat ride that adds to the appeal of the island experience. From Faro's marina, several boat cruises run that provide a leisurely journey across the Ria Formosa with the chance to see wildlife along the route. You can walk the island's trails and beaches once you get there.

Ilha Deserta is the perfect getaway for anyone looking for peace, beauty, and a sense of escape. It is a truly hidden sanctuary within the Ria Formosa Natural Park, allowing tourists to detach from the outer world and immerse themselves in the beauty of nature thanks to its beautiful beaches, unspoiled landscapes, and tranquil ambiance.

Ilha da Culatra: A Fishing Community's Haven

The enchanting island of Ilha da Culatra, which is a part of the Ria Formosa Natural Park, provides a fascinating look at the customary way of life of a fishing village. This island is a sanctuary for anyone looking for an authentic and off-the-beaten-path experience with its beautiful streets, colourful homes, and immaculate beaches.

The following are some reasons to visit Ilha da Culatra:

1. Culatra, a bustling fishing community, is located on the island of Ilha da Culatra. You'll get a chance to see how the island's fishermen go about their everyday lives and learn about their enduring customs as you tour the place. The community gives off an air of genuineness and provides a direct window into the Algarve's fishing history.

2. **Narrow Streets & Colourful Houses:** Take in the lovely sceneries as you stroll around Culatra's streets, where colourful homes are decorated with fishing nets, brilliant flowers, and painted murals. You are enticed to meander and find hidden places at your leisure by the beautiful ambiance created by the winding lanes and

cobblestone pathways. The architecture of the village is simple and lovely, which adds to its attractiveness.

3. Culatra Beach is a must-see attraction that stretches along the island's coastline. This long, sandy beach, which is bordered by crystal-clear waters and dunes, provides a serene and picturesque location for swimming, sunbathing, and just taking in the peace. The beach is conveniently located near the village and offers a stunning natural setting.

4. **Fresh Seafood**: A trip to Ilha da Culatra wouldn't be complete without indulging in some of the fresh seafood the island has to offer. Delicious dishes cooked with locally caught fish and seafood are served in many of the island's cafes and restaurants. A unique gastronomic experience, seafood

specialties made traditionally let you enjoy the flavours of the Algarve.

5. **Lighthouse and scenic views:** The Farol da Culatra, a lighthouse that serves as the island's emblem, is located near the eastern end of the island.

For sweeping views of the surrounding Ria Formosa, the nearby islands, and the huge Atlantic Ocean, climb to the top of the lighthouse. The views are especially beautiful at daybreak or sunset, providing a magnificent setting for special occasions.

6. **Birdwatching and nature trails**: Ilha da Culatra is a haven for those who love the outdoors. You can travel across dunes, marshes, and salt pans by taking one of the many nature routes that traverse the island. These routes

provide chances to view the rich variety of flora and fauna on the island as well as many bird species that call the Ria Formosa home. The area is home to a large variety of migratory and coastal species, which birdwatchers will enjoy spotting.

Visitors can travel back in time and engage with the fishing culture of the Algarve at Ilha da Culatra, which offers an authentic and immersive experience. This island offers a tranquil and satisfying respite from the busy mainland thanks to its beautiful settlement, gorgeous beaches, and natural beauty, making it the perfect location for those looking for an off-the-beaten-path adventure.

Ilha da Faro: Sun, Sand, and Serenity

The gorgeous island of Ilha de Faro, which sits off the coast of Faro, is a wonderful combination of the outdoors, fun activities, and easy access to the city. It's the perfect place to go if you're looking for peace, sun, and tranquillity because of its pristine beaches, calm environment, and breathtaking coastal views. What makes Ilha da Faro a must-see location is listed below:

1. Ilha da Faro is well known for its stunning sandy beaches. Long lengths of the island's golden sand and its crystal-clear seas offer a tranquil and welcoming setting for activities like swimming, sunbathing, and going to the beach.

   The beaches are kept up properly and provide amenities like beach bars, showers, and umbrellas to make going to the beach enjoyable.

2. Ilha da Faro's proximity to the city of Faro is one of its distinctive features. A quick ferry ride or a short walk across the bridge from the mainland of Faro will get you to the island. This convenience makes it the perfect getaway for both tourists and locals because it enables visitors to combine their city sightseeing with a leisurely beach day.

3. **Family-Friendly Atmosphere**: Ilha de Faro is renowned for its welcoming atmosphere. Children can swim and play safely due to the calm seas and shallow regions. Building sandcastles, enjoying strolls along the shore, or indulging in a picnic on the beach are all enjoyable family activities. The serene ambiance of the island

contributes to the laid-back and comfortable ambiance.

4. **Watersports and Leisure Activities:** Ilha da Faro provides a variety of watersports and leisure activities for those looking for more active interests. You can rent a jet ski to tour the nearby waterways or try your hand at windsurfing, kayaking, paddleboarding, or any number of other water sports.

The island's calm sea air and crystal-clear seas make it the perfect setting for taking part in these thrilling outdoor pursuits.

5. Ilha de Faro has stunning natural scenery in addition to its beaches, making it a great place for nature walks and birdwatching. Enjoy a stroll through the dunes, coastal greenery, and salt pans that surround the island's

roads and trails. Since the island is a part of the Ria Formosa Natural Park and serves as a habitat for numerous bird species, nature lovers will appreciate the opportunities for birding.

6. **Beachside Dining:** Ilha de Faro has beachside cafes and restaurants where you may indulge in delectable regional fare when you're hungry. Enjoy mouthwatering Portuguese specialties, fresh seafood dishes, or just unwind with a cool beverage while admiring the breathtaking ocean views.

   The restaurants on the seaside offer a tranquil and gorgeous backdrop for an unforgettable dining experience.

A real jewel, Ilha de Faro blends tranquillity, ease of access, and natural beauty. Ilha de Faro offers the ideal setting for sun, sand,

and tranquillity just a short distance from Faro's city centre, whether you're looking to unwind on the beach, participate in water activities, or simply immerse yourself in the island's peaceful surroundings.

FARO'S CULTURAL HIGHLIGHTS

Faro Municipal Theater: A Stage for Art and Entertainment

The centrally placed Faro Municipal Theater serves as a thriving cultural centre, offering a wide variety of artistic acts and entertainment.

The theatre offers both locals and visitors an enriching experience with its distinctive architecture, cutting-edge amenities, and a wide schedule of activities. What makes Faro Municipal Theater a must-see location is as follows:

1. **Architectural Grace:** The theatre's architecture in and of itself is beautiful. Its neoclassical façade, which is embellished with exquisite columns

and delicate decorations, gives the cityscape a sense of grandeur. The elaborate ceilings, luxurious seats, and spectacular stage create an enticing and visually attractive ambiance within the theatre, which has a finely constructed interior.

2. The Faro Municipal Theater presents a wide range of theatrical works, such as plays, musicals, and dance acts. The stage is taken over by talented national and international performers, who deliver compelling performances of anything from modern plays to classic dramas.

The theatre's schedule offers something for everyone to enjoy by catering to a variety of tastes and interests.

3. **Concerts**: The theatre serves as a venue for a variety of musical performances, including classical, jazz, pop, and traditional Portuguese music. Famous performers, orchestras, and ensembles perform, showcasing their abilities and giving music lovers wonderful experiences.

   The theatre has an extensive musical calendar throughout the year, ranging from symphony concerts to private recitals.

4. **Dance Shows:** The wide variety of dance acts offered at the theatre will appeal to dance enthusiasts. There are performances of flamenco, modern dance, ballet, and other dance styles by both domestic and foreign dance companies. The theatre's stage serves as a venue for creative expression and movement-based storytelling,

capturing spectators with compelling performances.

5. **Comedy and Stand-Up Shows**: The Faro Municipal Theater presents comedy shows and stand-up performances for individuals looking for levity and pleasure. Famous comics take the stage and perform amazing performances that have the crowd in fits of laughter. These performances present an opportunity to relax, have a nice time, and take in a night of fun entertainment.

6. Beyond the performing arts, the theatre also conducts cultural activities and art exhibitions that honour photography, visual arts, and other artistic mediums. These shows give regional and local artists a venue to display their ability and give tourists a

peek into Faro's thriving arts community.

7. The Faro Municipal Theater is dedicated to community participation and provides seminars, educational programs, and cultural events for people of all ages. These programs seek to support creative expression, develop local talent, and promote involvement in the arts.

The theatre encourages creative and artistic growth via anything from children's programs to theatre workshops for aspiring performers.

You can completely immerse yourself in the city's cultural heritage by going to the Faro Municipal Theater. The theatre offers a venue for artistic expression and amusement, whether you're enthralled by theatrical productions, lured to the alluring melodies of a concert, or inspired by visual arts. Experience Faro's thriving cultural scene by attending one of the many events scheduled at this legendary location.

Capela dos Ossos: The Chapel of Bones

Faro is home to Capela dos Ossos, often referred to as the Chapel of Bones, a singular and fascinating tourist destination. Visitors can have a thought-provoking experience while seeing this gruesome but interesting chapel, which has a huge historical significance for the city. What makes Capela dos Ossos a must-see location is as follows:

1. **Historical Significance**: Capela dos Ossos, a portion of the Church of Nossa Senhora do Carmo, was constructed in the 19th century. The chapel was built to serve as a sombre reminder of both the transient quality of existence and the inevitable nature of death.

   It was created as a space for introspection and thought, highlighting the transience and frailty of human life.

2. **Bone Decorations**: Capela dos Ossos' interior, which is fully covered in human bones and skulls, is its most stunning feature. The chapel's walls and pillars are covered in artfully arranged bone remains, making for an unsettling yet fascinating spectacle. More than 1,000 monks' bones are thought to have been used to decorate the church.

3. **Religious Symbolism:** Capela dos Ossos is a place of religious significance despite its macabre look. The chapel intends to provoke visitors' meditation on the transience of life and the value of spiritual reflection.

The chapel's religious decorations and altars seek to remind visitors of the spiritual side of life while the bones and skulls act as a reminder of the transience of the flesh.

4. **Complex Architecture:** Capela dos Ossos's architecture is renowned in and of itself. Beautiful arches, high ceilings, and elaborate tilework enhance the chapel's aesthetic appeal. A distinctive and thought-provoking ambiance is produced by the contrast between the elaborate building and the bone embellishments.

5. An intense and thought-provoking experience can be had by visiting Capela dos Ossos. It forces guests to consider their mortality and the fleeting essence of existence. The meditative ambiance of the chapel and the presence of human remains encourage introspection and a greater comprehension of the human predicament.

6. **Historical Context**: Capela dos Ossos sheds light on the customs and beliefs that prevailed at the time it was constructed. It provides a window into the time's attitudes and ideas on dying and the afterlife. Understanding the historical background helps people appreciate this special location and its importance to the neighbourhood.

Given that Capela dos Ossos has a significant religious and cultural significance for the local population, it is crucial to approach it with respect and understanding. Although it may not be for everyone, Capela dos Ossos is an exciting and unique place to visit if you have an interest in history, religious symbolism, and thought-provoking events.

Centro Cultural António Aleixo: Embracing Contemporary Art

Faro's Centro Cultural António Aleixo is a thriving cultural hub devoted to advancing and displaying modern art in all of its forms. The institution, which bears the name of the celebrated Portuguese poet and singer, offers a venue for both domestic and foreign artists to display their works and interact with the public. What makes Centro Cultural António Aleixo a must-see place for art lovers is as follows:

1. **Exhibitions of Contemporary Art:** The centre presents a recurring schedule of exhibitions of contemporary art, including creations by up-and-coming and well-known artists. These exhibitions feature a variety of artistic forms, including photography, installations, sculpture, painting, and more.

   Visitors can explore exhibitions that are visually stunning and thought-provoking while immersing themselves in the vibrant world of modern art.

2. **Local and foreign artists:** The Centro Cultural António Aleixo exhibits the

skills of both regionally-based Algarve artists and artists from all over the world. Visitors can experience a wide variety of artistic expressions in a stimulating atmosphere thanks to the diversity of artistic ideas and cultural influences. It provides a chance to come across fresh talent and learn about various artistic methods and themes.

3. **Cultural Events and Performances:** The centre offers a range of cultural events and performances in addition to visual arts. These could consist of musical performances, dancing performances, theatrical productions, poetry readings, and movie screenings.

The vibrant program enhances Faro's cultural landscape by giving people a venue for their creative expression and encouraging a sense of community involvement.

4. Art workshops and educational events are available at Centro Cultural António Aleixo to pique the interest of visitors of all ages and socioeconomic backgrounds. The hands-on art experiences offered by these programs enable participants to explore their creativity while being guided by seasoned artists.

The centre's educational programs are designed to encourage artistic growth and a passion for modern art.

5. **Community Engagement**: Through its outreach programs and activities, the cultural centre actively engages with the neighbourhood. It works in partnership with nearby schools, groups, and artists to support creative

expression and advance cultural understanding. Centro Cultural António Aleixo endeavours to foster artistic debate and exchange by bringing art to the community through exhibitions, seminars, and events.

6. **Architectural Grace:** The Centro Cultural António Aleixo's actual building is beautiful. The architecture of the building is sleek and contemporary, creating a beautiful backdrop for the artwork on show. The areas are carefully planned to improve the exhibition experience and foster a welcoming environment for guests to interact with modern art.

A journey into the realm of modern art can be had by visiting Centro Cultural António Aleixo. The centre offers a venue for artistic expression, cultural engagement, and social interaction through compelling exhibitions and exciting cultural activities. This Faro cultural centre offers a chance to accept and enjoy the variety and inventiveness of contemporary art, whether you're an art connoisseur or just looking for inspiration.

Cultural Festivals and Events

The dynamic city of Faro, which is located in Portugal's Algarve area, is well-known for its thriving cultural scene and a wide variety of annual festivals and events. Faro offers a diverse range of cultural experiences, from traditional festivals to modern art events. The following are some prominent festivals and events to keep an eye out for:

1. Festa do Ria Formosa is a well-liked yearly celebration of the rich cultural

history and scenic beauty of the Ria Formosa region. Live music performances, traditional dances, art exhibits, and delectable cuisine are all part of this festival in Faro. It's a wonderful chance to become immersed in local customs and take in the Algarve's distinctive cultural environment.

2. **Festival F:** This energetic music festival, which takes place in Faro, brings together well-known local and foreign musicians for a weekend of live performances.

Rock, pop, electronic, and world music are just a few of the musical genres that are featured during the event. Festival F is a favourite among music lovers thanks to its several stages, dynamic performances, and lively environment.

3. One of the oldest fairs in Portugal, Feira de Santa Iria is an annual event that dates back to the 17th century. This annual event, which takes place in October, offers a variety of entertainment options, including amusement rides, food vendors, live music, and cultural displays.

It's a fun event for the whole family that combines culinary, cultural, and entertainment activities.

4. Theater Week, also known as Semana do Teatro, is a cultural celebration that promotes theatre and other performing arts in Faro. Several theatre productions, seminars, talks, and exhibitions are part of the week-long schedule. It's a wonderful chance to take in the city's thriving theatre

industry and see the artistic talent of regional theatre companies.

5. Beer lovers should put the Alameda Beer Fest, an annual craft beer event held in Faro, on their calendars. Visitors to this event can experience a wide array of uncommon flavours and styles of craft beers from regional and worldwide breweries. Beer enthusiasts will find it to be a lovely event thanks to live music, food vendors, and a welcoming ambiance.

6. **International Motorcycle Rally**: One of the biggest and most famous motorcycle events in Europe takes place in Faro. For this yearly event, which includes exhibitions, motorcycle displays, live music, and thrilling motorbike competitions, motorcycle lovers from all over the world congregate in Faro. It's an exciting

event that displays motorcyclists' camaraderie and love for motorcycles.

These are only a few instances of festivals and events of a cultural nature that take place in Faro. There is always something going on thanks to the city's thriving cultural scene, whether it's a music festival, a traditional market, an art exhibition, or a theatrical production.

When visiting Faro, make sure to look out for upcoming festivals and events that interest you in the area's event listings.

GASTRONOMIC DELIGHTS OF FARO

Exploring Faro's Culinary Scene

Faro, a city in Portugal's Algarve area that boasts a vibrant and savoury culinary scene, is a foodies' delight. The region's rich culinary legacy is on display in the city's restaurants, cafes, and markets, which serve both traditional Portuguese cuisine and flavours from around the world.

Here are some highlights of Faro's gastronomic offerings that you should check out:

1. **Fresh Seafood:** Faro is well-known for its fresh seafood because it is a coastal city. You can choose from a wide variety of delectable seafood alternatives in the city's eateries, such as grilled sardines and sweet prawns.

Don't pass up the chance to sample regional delicacies like percebes (goose barnacles), which are regarded as a delicacy in the area, or cataplana (a seafood stew cooked in a copper clam-shaped pot).

2. Faro is the starting point for Algarvian cuisine, which is renowned for its straightforward but tasty meals that emphasise seasonal ingredients. Try traditional fare like Xarém (a corn-based dish with seafood or beef), Cataplana de Peixe (fish cooked in a cataplana), and Arroz de Marisco (seafood rice). These recipes frequently contain items like olives, almonds, figs, and olive oil that is grown nearby.

3. Visit the Mercado Municipal (Municipal Market) in Faro for a genuine culinary experience. Fresh fruits, vegetables, meats, and seafood are among the

many fresh produce options available at this bustling market. Local goods like cheeses, cured meats, and customary pastries are also available. Investigate the marketplace, talk to the sellers, and get some supplies to make your culinary treats.

4. **Pasteis de Nata**: The renowned Pasteis de Nata, a traditional Portuguese custard tart, must be indulged in during every trip to Portugal. These delicious pastries can be found all across Faro at cafes and pastry shops. Enjoy them as a delicious treat at the end of a meal or with a cup of coffee.

5. **Wine tasting**: The Algarve region is renowned for its wines, and Faro provides an opportunity for wine enthusiasts to partake in tastings and discover the regional wine industry. To taste Algarvian wines, including whites,

reds, and rosés, visit wine bars and wine cellars in the city. Some places even provide guided tastings so you may learn about the aromas and peculiarities of the wines from the area.

6. **International Cuisine**: Faro is a city with a diverse population, and this is reflected in its culinary offerings. A variety of international cuisines are available, including Indian, Italian, Mediterranean, and more. Discover hidden gems and one-of-a-kind dining experiences that suit a variety of tastes and preferences by exploring the streets and neighbourhoods.

7. **Classic Desserts**: Indulge in some of Faro's classic desserts. A delicious dessert made with almonds, egg yolks, and sugar is called Dom Rodrigo. Morgado is a confection created with

marzipan, figs, and almonds. These sweets give you a delicious sample of the area's sweet customs.

Remember to relish the flavours, embrace the regional traditions, and take in the laid-back dining culture when visiting Faro's food scene. Faro provides a wide variety of gastronomic experiences that will give you a deeper understanding of the cuisine of the Algarve, from seafood delicacies to traditional desserts.

Traditional Algarvian Dishes to Try

Be sure to try some of the typical Algarvian delicacies that highlight the region's distinctive flavours and culinary traditions while in Faro and touring the Algarve. You should try these delectable Algarvian dishes:

1. **Cataplana de Marisco**: Cataplana de Marisco is a traditional seafood meal from the Algarve, and it is full of taste. It is made up of a variety of fresh seafood, including fish, clams, mussels, and prawns, which are prepared with white wine, onions, tomatoes, garlic, herbs, and other seasonings.

   The name of the dish comes from the cataplana, a characteristic clam-shaped copper cooking pot used to traditionally boil the ingredients, producing a flavorful and aromatic seafood stew.

2. **Arroz de Marisco:** This traditional Algarvian dish exemplifies the region's love of rice and seafood. A variety of fresh shellfish, including prawns, clams, mussels, and occasionally fish or squid, are used to make this delectable seafood rice dish. A wonderful and

fragrant dish is produced by cooking the rice in a rich broth that has been flavoured with saffron, garlic, onions, and tomatoes.

3. **Amêijoas à Bulho Pato:** Clams are prepared in a straightforward yet tasty manner in this well-known Algarvian meal. The dish that results from swiftly cooking the clams in olive oil, garlic, coriander, and a little bit of white wine brings out the flavours of the shellfish. The tasty soup can be soaked up by the crusty bread that is frequently offered with it.

4. Cataplana de Peixe is a fish dish made with a variety of fish, potatoes, tomatoes, onions, garlic, herbs, and white wine. This meal, like Cataplana de Marisco, is prepared in a traditional cataplana pot, which allows the

ingredients to combine and produce a substantial and fragrant seafood stew.

5. Goose barnacles, also known as percebes, are a delicacy in the Algarve. These distinctive seafood specialties are gathered from the area's rugged coasts. Normally, percebes are served cooked and with a squeeze of lemon. They are a great delicacy for seafood lovers thanks to their particular flavour and slightly salty taste.

6. **Sardinhas Assadas:** Sardinhas Assadas, also known as grilled sardines, is a popular Algarvian meal that pays homage to the area's long history of fishing. Fish that is delicate and tasty is produced when fresh sardines are grilled over an open flame while being seasoned with coarse sea salt. This recipe is a must-try during the summer when sardines are in season and is

served with a squeeze of lemon, a side of lettuce, and crusty bread.

7. **Carne de Porco à Alentejana**: Although not just eaten in the Algarve, this meal is popular all over Portugal, including the country's Algarve area. It includes clams, garlic, paprika, white wine, and tender pork cubes that have been marinated. Pork and clams combine their distinct flavours to make a tasty and fulfilling dish.

These are just a few instances of the regional cuisine's rich culinary heritage found in traditional Algarvian dishes. Enjoy these savoury and original dishes when in Faro or the Algarve to fully appreciate the distinctive flavours of the area.

Seafood Extravaganza: Fresh Catches and Delicacies

Faro and the Algarve region provide a veritable cornucopia of fresh catches and delicacies when it comes to seafood. Due to its seaside position, the area is well known for its plethora of seafood options. Here are some of the seafood dishes you simply must taste while there:

1. **Fresh Sardines Grilled:** Grilled sardines, also known as "sardines asanas," are a traditional dish in the Algarve, especially in the summer. Enjoy the simplicity of grilled to perfection, sea salt-seasoned, tender, and juicy sardines. These delicious fish are an absolute treat when served with a splash of lemon.

2. **Cataplana de Marisco:** This seafood lover's paradise is Cataplana de

Marisco. A variety of fresh seafood, including clams, mussels, prawns, and fish, are combined in this flavorful dish and cooked with onions, tomatoes, garlic, herbs, and white wine. A rich and savoury seafood stew is produced by cooking the ingredients in a traditional copper cataplana pot, which allows the flavours to merge.

3. **Arroz de Marisco:** Arroz de Marisco is a traditional seafood rice dish from Portugal. This filling and delectable dish blends rice with a variety of fresh seafood, including clams, mussels, fish, and even squid. This tasty recipe exemplifies the Algarve's love of fish and rice and is seasoned with saffron, garlic, onions, tomatoes, and white wine.

4. Clams are cooked in olive oil, garlic, coriander, and a little bit of white wine

in the dish known as "Ameijoas à Bulho Pato," which is straightforward but fragrant. A delectable broth is produced by combining fresh clams with the fragrant tastes of garlic and coriander. To enjoy every flavorful sip of the soup, dunk some crusty bread into it.

5. Goose barnacles, also known as percebes, are a distinctive and highly sought-after seafood delicacy in the Algarve. These odd-looking shellfish, which are taken from the rocky shorelines, have a delicate, somewhat saline flavour. Percebes are a real pleasure for lovers of seafood when they are boiled and served with a squeeze of lemon.

6. **Polvo à Lagareiro**: Tender octopus cooked to perfection is the star of this traditional dish. After being boiled until

fork-tender, the octopus is then roasted in the oven with garlic, olive oil, and sea salt. The result is a delicious dish that highlights the octopus's natural flavour.

7. **Seafood Cataplana:** In addition to the above-stated traditional cataplana recipes, you may also get seafood cataplana varieties that combine fish, prawns, clams, and other delectable shellfish. A delicious potpourri of flavours is produced when these meals are cooked with a delectable combination of herbs, tomatoes, onions, and white wine.

8. **Fresh Shellfish:** Take advantage of the chance to savour fresh shellfish including prawns, langoustines, and crab. These delicacies highlight the beautiful tastes and textures of the sea,

whether they are served simply boiled or as part of a seafood platter.

Visit neighbourhood seafood restaurants, beachside cafés, and seafood markets to sample the freshness and variety of the area's catches while exploring the seafood fiesta in Faro and the Algarve. The seafood options in the Algarve will provide you with a remarkable and delicious gastronomic experience, from grilled delicacies to hearty stews.

DAY TRIPS FROM FARO

Tavira: The Jewel of the Eastern Algarve

Tavira, a town in Portugal's Eastern Algarve, is frequently referred to as the region's crown jewel due to the way it enchants tourists with its historic allure, natural beauty, and cultural diversity.

This charming town offers a lovely fusion of history, architecture, and natural beauty. It is located along the banks of the Gila River. Here are some reasons to visit Tavira:

1. **Historic core**: Tavira's historic core is a beautifully maintained wealth of historical value and stunning architecture. You can find exquisite whitewashed cottages, delicately carved entrances, and vibrant facades covered in traditional tiles as you stroll

along its winding, cobblestone lanes. Don't pass up the chance to visit sites that provide a window into the town's colourful past, like the Santa Maria do Castelo Church and the Tavira Castle Ruins.

2. **Roman Bridge**: The Ponte Romana, also referred to as the Roman Bridge, is a well-known landmark in Tavira. This historic bridge, built over the Gilo River, offers breathtaking views of the town and a charming setting for strolls. You can enter the town's magical ambiance by taking a stroll across the bridge.

3. **Historic Churches:** Tavira is renowned for its stunning, individually charming churches. Take a look at the Igreja da Misericórdia's beautiful Manueline doorway and stunning azulejo tiles. Another must-see is the Igreja de Santa

Maria do Castelo, which is housed amid the Tavira Castle's ruins and has Gothic and Renaissance-style architecture. The religious and cultural history of the town may be seen in these churches.

4. Visit the museums and cultural institutions of Tavira to fully immerse yourself in the local culture. The Tavira Municipal Museum displays the history, archaeology, and art of the city and is located in the ancient Convento da Graça from the sixteenth century.

The history of the area's Moors is revealed in the Ncleo Islamico Museum. These cultural landmarks help us comprehend Tavira's diverse cultural heritage better.

5. **Ilha de Tavira**: This gorgeous barrier island, which stretches down the coast,

is only a short boat ride from the town. The island provides a calm haven with its clean sandy beaches, clear waters, and relaxed atmosphere. Explore the island's natural sceneries, which include dunes and salt pans, or unwind on the beach or in the sea.

6. **Ria Formosa Natural Park**: The protected region known for its varied ecosystems and birdlife, the Ria Formosa Natural Park, is also accessible from Tavira. To see the splendour of this seaside haven, take a boat tour or a trek around the park's paths.

For nature lovers and birdwatchers, the salt pans, marshlands, and lagoons of the park provide a breathtaking backdrop.

7. Tavira's culinary scene is a delight for food enthusiasts. Enjoy delectable pastries, traditional Algarvian fare, and delicious fish dishes. The town's various eateries, coffee shops, and local markets provide a wide range of culinary experiences that highlight the local flavours and culinary customs.

Tavira's rich history, stunning architecture, breathtaking scenery, and friendly people all contribute to its allure. Tavira guarantees an exciting voyage through the alluring history of the Eastern Algarve, whether you choose to explore the historic town, relax on Ilha de Tavira, or immerse yourself in the cultural treasures.

Lagos: Historic Port Town and Stunning Beaches

Lagos, a captivating town in Portugal's Western Algarve, is well-known for its enthralling past, gorgeous surroundings, and stunning beaches. This seaside jewel is a must-visit location for tourists since it perfectly combines natural beauty and cultural legacy. Here are some reasons Lagos stands out as a unique location to visit:

1. **Historic Centre**: The historic centre of Lagos is a veritable architectural and historical treasure trove. You'll come across centuries-old structures, elaborate churches, and attractive squares as you stroll through its winding, cobbled alleys.

    Don't pass up the chance to see famous sites like the Santo António Church from the 17th century, the old Lagos

Fortress, and the breathtaking Igreja de Sao Sebastiao with its tiled front.

2. **Lagos Marina:** This bustling centre combines maritime activities with a fun environment. A stroll down the marina will reveal a variety of vibrant boats, cafes, and eateries. The marina serves as a starting point for several boat tours and aquatic activities, including dolphin watching and exploring the breathtaking coastline, in addition to being a lovely location.

3. **Ponta da Piedade**: Just south of Lagos, there lies a natural wonder called Ponta da Piedade. This amazing rock structure has towering cliffs, secret caverns, and blue waters that are extremely pure. To get to the stunning beaches hidden within the cliffs, either take a boat tour or walk down the steps. The clifftop panoramas are

incredibly magnificent and provide a singular viewpoint of the Algarve's coastline splendour.

4. **Lagos Slave Market**: The Lagos Slave Market is a reminder of Lagos' important historical ties to the Age of Discovery. This museum investigates the town's function as a hub for the trade of African slaves in the 15th and 16th centuries. Visitors can learn about this terrible period of history and how it affected the area through exhibits and presentations.

5. **Lagos Walls:** The historic Roman walls that encircle Lagos are in good condition. The town's walls once provided protection, but today they provide a chance to stroll up the ramparts and take in expansive views of both the town and the beach. The walls offer a unique view of Lagos'

historic layout as well as a window into the town's colourful past.

6. **Beaches in Lagos**: Lagos is endowed with some of the Algarve's most beautiful beaches. Praia Dona Ana is frequently cited as one of Portugal's most stunning beaches because of its golden cliffs and clean waves.

   Long sandy beaches can be found in Meia Praia, but Praia do Camilo draws people in with its secret cove and striking rock formations. These beaches offer wonderful locations for swimming, water sports, and tanning.

A compelling fusion of history, the outdoors, and the seashore can be found in Lagos. Lagos guarantees a fascinating trip through the distinct heritage and alluring landscapes of the Western Algarve, whether you choose to explore the town's ancient centre, savour the magnificent beaches, or venture outside to find the local natural wonders.

Silves: A Glimpse into the Algarve's Moorish Past

Silves, a charming village in Portugal's central Algarve region, provides a fascinating look into the area's Moorish heritage. For anyone interested in learning more about the cultural history of the Algarve, Silves is a must-visit location because of its extensive history, stunning architecture, and attractive surroundings.

The following reasons make Silves stand out as a unique location to visit:

1. **Silves Castle**: Also referred to as Castelo de Silves, Silves Castle is a

notable structure that dominates the town's skyline. The strategic importance of Silves during the Moorish era is attested to by this mediaeval fortification. Explore the impressive structure's well-preserved walls, towers, and cisterns as you try to imagine the history that once took place there. The town and the surrounding countryside may be seen in breathtaking detail from the castle.

2. **Silves Cathedral:** The magnificent Gothic Silves Cathedral, or Sé de Silves, represents the historical importance of the town.

   The cathedral, which was constructed on the site of a mediaeval mosque, displays a fusion of Christian and Moorish architectural influences. Admire the rose window, gorgeous interior, and fine religious relics it houses, as well as the magnificent stonework. A representation of Silves' spiritual and cultural history is the cathedral.

3. **Archaeological Museum:** With its substantial collection of relics, the Silves Municipal Archaeological Museum sheds light on the town's past.

   Discover the different cultural influences that have shaped Silves by looking at ancient pottery, Roman antiquities, and Islamic ceramics. The museum's displays let visitors have a deeper understanding of the past and the significance of the area across many eras of history.

4. Silves' old district is a beautiful place to explore. Take a stroll down its winding alleyways surrounded by whitewashed homes decorated with vibrant tiles and

classic chimneys. Find charming squares, classic cafes, and neighbourhood stores that provide a window into life in this old town. The town's Moorish and mediaeval past are reflected in the architectural elements and lively atmosphere.

5. **River Arade**: Silves' location along the river's banks adds to the city's natural beauty. Take a stroll down the riverfront promenade to take in the serene atmosphere and see the stunning views of the river and the surrounding area. To appreciate the natural beauty and see Silves from a different angle, you may also take a boat tour along the river.

6. Summertime brings Silves its annual Medieval Festival, which brings the town's past to life. With costumed performers, jousting contests,

traditional music, and mouthwatering food, the event turns the streets into a bustling mediaeval village. Enjoy the historical reenactments, take part in the festive atmosphere, and immerse yourself in the celebration of Silves' mediaeval heritage.

Silves, with its imposing castle, ancient church, and rich cultural legacy, provides an enthralling voyage into the Moorish past of the Algarve.

Silves promises an educational experience that peels back the layers of the area's cultural tapestry, whether you're taking in the mediaeval festival, touring the town's architectural wonders, or learning about its history at the archaeological museum.

Sagres: Where Land Ends and Adventure Begins

The city of Sagres, which sits on the southwest coast of Portugal, epitomises the spirit of exploration and adventure. Sagres, which is well-known for its untamed coastline, breathtaking cliffs, and historical significance, provides a singular experience where land and water converge.

Here are some reasons to visit Sagres if you're an adventurer:

1. The southwestmost point of Europe is marked by Cape St. Vincent, also known as Cabo de São Vicente, a spectacular headland. You can see breathtaking panoramic vistas and magnificent sunsets while standing on the cliffs overlooking the Atlantic Ocean. The cape is notable historically

because it served as a key navigational hub during the Age of Discovery.

2. Sagres fortification, also known as Fortaleza de Sagres, is a mediaeval fortification that was significant to Portugal's naval history. Discover the fort's walls, towers, and the renowned Rose of the Winds compass, which Prince Henry the Navigator is reputed to have created. The fortress provides a window into Sagres' strategic significance throughout the age of exploration.

3. **Ponta da Atalaia**: This breathtaking vantage point offers a spectacular view of the rocky coastline and pounding surf. Awe and adventure are evoked by the captivating vista of the Atlantic Ocean from this natural viewing point. Photographers and nature lovers can

capture the breathtaking seaside scenery of Sagres here.

4. **Watersports and Surfing**: Sagres is known for having outstanding surf conditions that draw surfers from all over the world. It provides perfect conditions for surfers of all skill levels with its strong waves and steady swells. In addition to surfing, the area's windy environment and picturesque shoreline are perfect for other water activities including windsurfing, kitesurfing, and paddleboarding.

5. Sagres is a top spot for bird watching because it is situated near migratory paths. Falcons, eagles, and seabirds are just a few of the bird species that are drawn to the area's cliffs and coastal settings. To see these gorgeous creatures in their native environment,

birdwatchers might explore the cliffs, beaches, and nature preserves.

6. **Nature Trails and Trekking**: Sagres is a great starting point for trekking and exploring the surrounding natural splendour. See the stunning views of the coastline from the pathways that wind along the cliffs. Sagres is located along the Rota Vicentina, a long-distance hiking track that provides access to the breathtaking natural scenery of the area.

7. **Dolphin Watching**: Departing from Sagres, take a boat ride to see dolphins in their natural environment. Numerous species of dolphins can be seen in their natural habitat in the waters off the coast of Sagres when you are accompanied by knowledgeable guides.

With its untamed scenery, historical significance, and options for outdoor activities, Sagres attracts explorers. Sagres is a destination where the excitement of adventure awaits at every turn, whether you're exploring the towering cliffs, riding the waves, seeing wildlife, or simply taking in the breathtaking surroundings.

OUTDOOR ADVENTURES IN FARO

For outdoor adventure seekers and sports fans, Faro, a city in Portugal's Algarve, provides a variety of thrilling activities. Faro offers the opportunity to discover its beautiful landscapes and partake in exhilarating outdoor activities, from water sports and hiking paths to birdwatching and golfing. Here are some outdoor activities you may take part in in Faro:

1. Faro is a great place to go for water sports and other activities because of its coastal position. You can engage in sports like surfing, windsurfing, kitesurfing, paddleboarding, and kayaking regardless of your skill level.

    For fans of water sports, the area's excellent wind and wave conditions, beautiful beaches, and crystal-clear seas make for an amazing playground.

2. **Hiking Trails and Nature Walks**: For outdoor enthusiasts, Faro and its surroundings offer a range of hiking trails and nature walks. Discover the many ecosystems, like salt marshes, dunes, and lagoons, by exploring the Ria Formosa Natural Park and its network of paths. The trails provide chances to take in the quiet of nature while observing rare plants and animals.

3. Ria Formosa is a coastal wetland and nature reserve close to Faro, Portugal, and is a haven for birdwatchers. Explore the birding hides and observation sites dotted across the park with your binoculars in hand. Several bird species, including flamingos, herons, spoonbills, and

numerous migratory birds that make Ria Formosa their temporary home, should be observed.

4. **Algarve golfing**: The Algarve is recognized for its top-notch golf courses, and Faro provides an opportunity for players of all ability levels to enjoy the game. Play a round of golf while admiring the breathtaking ocean views and green, well-kept fairways that surround you. Faro is a golfer's paradise thanks to the area's pleasant environment and top-notch courses.

5. **Riding**: Go on an adventure while riding to explore Faro and its surroundings. Riding a bicycle down the shore allows you to explore the quaint coastal communities and take in the Algarve's breathtaking scenery. Further north, you may cycle through

scenic farmland, wineries, and typical Algarvian communities.

6. Riding a horse is a beautiful way to explore the landscape and coastline of the Algarve. All ages and ability levels can ride horses at one of the many equestrian facilities and stables in the area. Take a guided tour to discover the many landscapes, from rural trails to sandy beaches, and take advantage of the special perspective that horseback riding offers.

7. Water parks and theme parks are available for both families and thrill-seekers in Faro and the neighbouring areas. Spend a fun-filled day at one of the water parks, where you can splash around in pools, rest in lazy rivers, and slide down thrilling water slides. Alternately, go to theme parks that provide a variety of

attractions like rides, performances, and hands-on activities.

Outdoor activities in Faro offer chances to discover the area's scenic splendour, partake in exhilarating pursuits, and make priceless memories. Faro provides a wide variety of outdoor adventures to suit every interest and level of adventure, whether you're looking for water sports adrenaline, serene nature hikes, birdwatching chances, or a round of golf.

SHOPPING AND SOUVENIRS

Traditional Crafts and Artisanal Products

Like many other places in Portugal, Faro has a long history of fine craftsmanship and handmade goods. It may be a lot of fun to explore the regional crafts and find one-of-a-kind handmade things while also supporting regional artisans.

In Faro, you can discover the following traditional crafts and artisanal goods:

1. **Pottery**: Faro is no different from the rest of Portugal in having a strong pottery tradition. Visit local pottery studios and workshops to see the art in action. Faro's traditional pottery frequently has intricate patterns and

decorations, with the colours white and blue being popular pairings. Look for lovely bowls, plates, tiles, and ornamental items that highlight the area's rich ceramic tradition.

2. **Products made of cork**: Portugal is the world's top producer of cork, and Faro is a great site to learn more about this unusual substance. You may buy a wide range of cork products, including wallets, purses, coasters, and even fashion accessories like hats and jewellery, which make excellent mementos.

   Products made of cork are not only fashionable but also eco-friendly and long-lasting.

3. Jewellery made with filigree is fragile and requires careful soldering and precise wirework. The filigree jewellery

produced in Faro is well-known for showcasing the talent and artistry of regional craftspeople. Look for jewellery with delicate filigree designs on the earrings, necklaces, bracelets, and rings. These pieces frequently have traditional motifs derived from the environment and local culture.

4. Handwoven baskets and mats are another type of local heritage seen in Faro. These products frequently include elaborate weaving patterns manufactured from natural materials like reeds or straw.

Small decorative baskets to enormous, practical ones that are used for shopping or transporting beach supplies are all examples of baskets. Mats are ideal for giving your home a dash of old-world character.

5. The craft of embroidery has been around for generations and is currently done in Faro. Traditional Algarvian embroidery frequently uses geometric motifs and patterns that draw inspiration from the region's flora and fauna.

   Look for embroidered products including apparel, ornamental objects, and tablecloths. Each thread is evidence of the craftspeople's talent and attention to detail.

6. Faro and the Algarve region are well-known for their top-notch honey and preserves. Discover a vast selection of honey, including uncommon varieties like orange blossom or lavender, by perusing neighbourhood markets and shops. Sample handcrafted jams and jellies produced from regional fruits like figs

and oranges. These goods are wonderful presents or snacks to bring home.

7. **Leather Products**: Making leather is another historic craft in Portugal, and Faro is home to a variety of leather products. Look for locally manufactured leather shoes, wallets, belts, and purses to see the craftsmanship at work. Portuguese leather is renowned for its high calibre, sturdiness, and classic design.

Discover the traditional crafts and artisanal goods of the area by looking for local artisans, visiting craft markets, and browsing specialty shops while you explore Faro. You may support these artisans and take home one-of-a-kind, genuine souvenirs while also helping to preserve Faro's cultural history.

Local Markets and Shopping Districts

The Algarve region of Portugal's capital city, Faro, has many local markets and retail areas where you can go exploring, find one-of-a-kind goods to buy, and learn about the culture. Here are some locations to visit for a true shopping experience in Faro, from hectic markets to lovely shopping streets:

1. Mercado Municipal de Faro: Located in the centre of the city, the Mercado Municipal de Faro is a bustling market where you can get a taste of the local culture and find a range of fresh foods, regional goods, and traditional crafts.

   Visit the welcoming sellers as you peruse the stalls of fruits, vegetables, fish, meats, and spices. Regional delicacies like cheese, olives, honey, and traditional pastries are also available. The market is a terrific location to try and buy local foods as well as acquire one-of-a-kind trinkets.

2. **Feira de Faro**: On Saturdays, Largo de San Francisco, a neighbourhood close to the city centre, hosts the weekly Feira de Faro market. This bustling market sells a variety of commodities, such as apparel, handicrafts, home goods, plants, and more.

Enjoy the bustling atmosphere as you explore the stalls, haggle with the dealers, and find hidden jewels. In addition to being a place to buy, Feira de Faro offers visitors a chance to engage with residents and experience the area's long-standing market culture.

3. **Rua de Santo António**: Situated in Faro's ancient district, Rua de Santo

António is a beautiful shopping street. The shops, boutiques, and cafes lining this pedestrian boulevard provide a comfortable setting for wandering and shopping.

Discover the local fashion boutiques, shop for one-of-a-kind accessories, peruse the handmade goods, or just relax with a cup of coffee and take in the atmosphere of the city. A great location for leisurely browsing and finding hidden gems is Rua de Santo António.

4. **Baixa de Faro**: The city's central business district, or Baixa de Faro, is a vibrant region that blends dining, shopping, and entertainment. You may purchase apparel, shoes, accessories, and other items on the major shopping strip, Rua de Dom Francisco Gomes, which is lined with a variety of local

and foreign shops. Since they frequently conceal smaller boutiques and specialty stores, explore the side streets and alleyways that branch off from the main street. A bustling environment and a wide range of shopping alternatives can be found in Baixa de Faro.

5. Faro Retail Park is a contemporary shopping centre outside of the city that houses bigger retail establishments, supermarkets, and a movie theatre. With a variety of stores selling food, apparel, electronics, home goods, and other items, this location provides a pleasant shopping experience.

It's a terrific location to discover well-known companies and take advantage of a variety of dining, shopping, and entertainment choices.

6. Faro Shopping Center: Another well-liked shopping area in the city is Faro Shopping Center. It is home to a range of stores, including clothing stores, electronics merchants, beauty and wellness stores, and more, and is close to the airport.

The shopping complex offers a roomy, air-conditioned environment for shopping and has enough visitor parking.

Take the chance to meet people, learn about traditional crafts, try local fare, and find one-of-a-kind souvenirs while exploring Faro's local markets and retail areas. These locations provide an authentic shopping experience in the heart of the Algarve while also providing a window into the local culture.

Unique Souvenirs to Bring Home

When in Faro, you may pick up a selection of one-of-a-kind trinkets that perfectly encapsulate the spirit of the city and make for thoughtful presents or souvenirs. Here are some ideas for interesting mementos to take home from Faro:

1. **Products made of cork**: Faro provides a variety of cork products. Portugal is the world's top cork producer. Look for cork-made accessories including wallets, backpacks, coasters, keychains, and even clothing pieces. These goods are not only fashionable and environmentally friendly, but they also honour the rich cork tradition of the nation.

2. **Hand-Painted Tiles:** Azulejos, or hand-painted tiles, are a well-known Portuguese artistic style. Look for ornamental tiles with recognizable

patterns, vibrant images, or depictions of regional landmarks. These tiles will bring a bit of Portuguese flair to your home and can be used as coasters or wall art.

3. **Portuguese Pottery**: Look around your neighbourhood for authentic Portuguese ceramics at pottery studios and workshops. Intricately patterned and colourful decorative tiles, bowls, vases, and other finely crafted items are what you should seek out. Portugal's extensive ceramic legacy is reflected in its craftsmanship and distinctive designs.

4. **Traditional Sardine Tin**: The sardine is a well-known culinary and cultural icon of Portugal. Pick up a classic sardine can that is decorated with vibrant paintings of sardines, regional motifs, or Portuguese customs. These tins can

be displayed as ornamental objects or utilised as storage containers.

5. **Traditional Food and Drink:** Choose regional foods and beverages to bring the flavours of Faro home. Try to find things like Portuguese olive oil, regional honey, jellies, and preserves, or a bottle of wine or liquor. You can continue to enjoy the flavours of the Algarve long after your trip thanks to these delectable treats.

6. **Jewellery made of filigree**: This intricate craftsmanship is a hallmark of traditional Portuguese jewellery. Think of buying a piece of filigree jewellery, such as earrings, necklaces, or bracelets, reflecting the country's cultural tradition and boasting exquisite motifs. These classic items make for tasteful and significant keepsakes.

7. **Handmade Items:** Faro is renowned for its handmade items. Try to find items that are handmade, such as leather goods, embroidered clothing, woven baskets, or wooden carvings. Each item in this collection embodies a distinct aspect of Faro's cultural identity and showcases the talent and creativity of local artists.

8. Portuguese traditional soaps are renowned for their exquisite scents. Look for classic Portuguese soaps with lavender, almond, or citrus scents that are manufactured with natural ingredients. These soaps provide a lovely sensory experience in addition to being useful keepsakes.

Don't forget to browse regional markets, artisan shows, and specialised stores to find these one-of-a-kind gifts. You may carry back a bit of Faro's history and make enduring memories of your trip to the Algarve by supporting regional craftsmen and buying genuine goods.

PRACTICAL TIPS AND RESOURCES

Safety and Emergency Information

Prioritise your safety and be ready for any emergencies that might occur when travelling to Faro or any other location. For your reference, the following is some crucial safety and emergency information:

1. Keep your personal belongings secure and be aware of your surroundings, especially in crowded places or popular tourist destinations, according to general safety advice.

2. Use reputable ride-sharing apps, authorised taxis, or trustworthy transportation providers.

3. When it's hot outside, remember to stay hydrated and wear sunscreen to shield yourself from the sun's rays.

4. Respect regional customs and laws as well as local laws and regulations.

5. Learn the local emergency phone numbers, such as those for the police, ambulance, and fire departments.

6. **Medical Emergencies:** To contact emergency services in Portugal in the event of a medical emergency, dial the emergency number 112.

7. Hospitals, clinics, and pharmacies are among the medical facilities in Faro. Keep a handy list of the closest hospitals and their phone numbers.

8. Having travel insurance that pays for medical costs and, if necessary,

emergency medical evacuation is advised.

9. **Personal Safety**: Exercise caution when using ATMs and keep significant sums of cash hidden from view.

10. Passports, identity cards, and other valuables should be kept in a safe location, such as a hotel safe.

11. Tell someone about your vacation schedules and plans, like a family member or trusted friend.

12. When out at night, stick to well-lit, busy locations and, if at all feasible, consider walking in groups.

13. **Natural disasters**: The Algarve region of Portugal occasionally experiences natural disasters like wildfires or hurricanes. Pay attention to weather

reports in your area, and heed any advice or directions given by local authorities.

14. If you are in a disaster-affected area, heed the advice of local authorities, take refuge in designated areas if necessary, and keep informed through reliable sources of information.

Information about the Embassy and travel documents:

- Maintain copies of crucial documents electronically or with a reliable contact while keeping your travel documents, including your passport, in a secure location.

- Learn the location and phone numbers of your country's embassy or consulate in Portugal in case you want assistance while there.

Keep in mind that this information should only be used as a broad guide, and it is always advisable to be aware of the local safety and emergency procedures before travelling. You can contribute to making sure that your vacation to Faro is safe and enjoyable by taking the essential precautions, being aware of your surroundings, and being organised.

Useful Phrases and Language Tips

While many people in Faro and the Algarve region speak English, knowing a few basic Portuguese phrases can greatly enhance your travel experience and help you connect with locals. Here are some useful phrases and language tips to keep in mind:

Greetings and Basic Expressions:

- Hello: Olá (oh-LAH)

- Good morning: Bom dia (BOHM DEE-ah)
- Good afternoon: Boa tarde (BOH-ah TAHR-deh)
- Good evening: Boa noite (BOH-ah NOY-teh)
- Thank you: Obrigado (for males) / Obrigada (for females) (oh-bree-GAH-doo/dah)
- Please: Por favor (poor fah-VOHR)
- Yes: Sim (seem) / No: Não (now)

Basic Conversation:

- Do you speak English?: Fala inglês? (FAH-lah een-GLAYS?)
- I don't understand: Não entendo (NOW en-TEN-doh)
- Excuse me: Com licença (kohm lee-SEN-sah)
- I'm sorry: Desculpe (dess-KOOL-peh)
- Can you help me?: Pode ajudar-me? (POH-deh ah-JOO-dahr-meh?)

Ordering Food and Drinks:

- I would like...: Eu gostaria de... (ayoo gos-TAH-ree-ah deh...)

- A table for [number of people], please: Uma mesa para [number of people], por favor (OO-mah MEH-zah PAH-rah [number of people], poor fah-VOHR)

- What do you recommend?: O que você recomenda? (oh keh voh-seh reh-koh-MEHN-dah?)

- The bill, please: A conta, por favor (ah KON-tah, poor fah-VOHR)

Getting Around:

- Where is...?: Onde fica...? (OHN-deh FEE-kah...?)
- How much does it cost?: Quanto custa? (KWAN-toh KOOSH-tah)

- Where is the nearest...?: Onde fica o(a) mais próximo(a)...? (OHN-deh FEE-kah oh/ah MAH-ees proh-SEE-moo/ah...?)

Emergency Phrases:

- Help!: Socorro! (soh-KOHR-roh!)
- I need a doctor: Preciso de um médico (preh-ZEE-zoo deh oom MEH-dee-koo)
- Where is the hospital?: Onde fica o hospital? (OHN-deh FEE-kah oh oh-SPY-tahl?)

Although English is widely spoken in Faro and the Algarve region, learning a few simple Portuguese phrases will tremendously improve your trip and help you interact with locals. Here are some language and phrase suggestions to remember:

Always remember to smile and use courteous gestures when you greet people since it conveys respect and warmth. Portuguese pronunciation may vary from English pronunciation, so give it some time, and don't be hesitant to ask for clarification if you need it.

During your stay in Faro, learning a few fundamental phrases in the native tongue will greatly improve your conversations and help you establish rapport. Even if you don't speak Portuguese well, the locals will respect your effort.

Recommended Websites and Apps

Website: www.visitalgarve.pt VisitFaro

- VisitFaro, the region's official tourism website, offers useful details on sights to see, things to do, places to stay, events, and helpful travel advice. It's a fantastic tool for organising your schedule and keeping up with local news and events.

Available on iOS and Android, Google Maps

- A dependable navigation program, Google Maps provides accurate maps, directions, and traffic updates. You may use it to get around Faro, locate restaurants, attractions, and other areas of interest, as well as alternatives for public transit.

Available on iOS and Android, the Moovit app

- An efficient app for public transportation called Moovit offers the most recent details on bus routes, schedules, and actual arrivals and departures.

You may use it to efficiently plan your trips and navigate the Faro area bus system.

Visit TripAdvisor at www.tripadvisor.com.

- Popular travel website TripAdvisor provides reviews, ratings, and suggestions made by users for lodging, dining, activities, and other services. It can be a useful tool for discovering top-rated places to stay and getting advice from other travellers.

www.weather.com is the website address.

- Planning your activities in Faro requires looking up the weather forecast. You can make appropriate preparations with the accurate weather data provided by Weather.com, including temperature, precipitation, and forecasts for the next few days.

(App: accessible for iOS and Android) Xplore Faro

- Xplore Faro is a thorough travel software that offers details on sights, tours, dining, shopping, and other aspects of Faro.

  It is a useful tool for touring the city because it comes with interactive maps, audio instructions, and carefully selected itineraries.

Download the Duolingo app for iOS or Android.

- Duolingo is a well-known language-learning program if you're interested in learning or practising Portuguese. It provides brief courses, activities, and tests to help you improve your language proficiency and interact more successfully with native speakers.

These online resources and mobile applications can improve your trip to Faro by giving you useful information, facilitating navigation, and guiding your decision-making.

Remember to verify reviews, confirm information, and utilise them as additional resources in addition to guidebooks and personal recommendations from the area.

Additional Travel Resources

Website: www.faroairport.com, Faro Airport

- Information on flights, modes of transportation, amenities, and services may be found on the Faro Airport's official website.

    It's a useful tool for organising the logistics of your arrival and departure.

Tourism Board of the Algarve (website: www.visitalgarve.pt)

- Faro and other sites in the Algarve region are thoroughly covered by the region's official tourism organisation. It offers information on places to visit, things to do, places to stay, events, and helpful travel advice.

Council of the City of Faro (www.cm-faro.pt)

- The Faro Civic Council's website has helpful information about civic initiatives, cultural events, and local government services.

  It can assist you to gain insight into the neighbourhood and keep you up to date on current events and urban development.

The website for Faro Public Transportation is www.emafaro.pt.

- The Faro Municipal Bus Companies (EMAF) website provides details on the times, prices, and tickets for local bus routes. It's an excellent tool for organising your travel within the city and its environs.

Visit Portugal's website for further information.

- Faro and other locations in Portugal are covered in great detail on the country's official tourism website.

  It provides details on Portuguese attractions, activities, lodging, and useful travel advice.

The online community at www.faro-expat.com/forum: Faro Forum

- In the online community known as the Faro Forum, you can meet other travellers, expats, and locals.

  It serves as a forum for discussing issues about Faro and the Algarve region as well as for sharing knowledge and advice.

Travel blogs and articles for Faro

- Numerous travel blogs and guides concentrate on Faro and the Algarve and provide first-hand accounts, suggestions, and advice from visitors who have visited the area. The information and ideas on these sites can help you organise your schedule.

Always make sure you're using reliable websites and getting information from multiple sources while using online resources. To acquire a comprehensive understanding of Faro and make the most of your vacation, it's helpful to combine online resources with guidebooks, local suggestions, and travellers' insights.

CONCLUSION

Reflecting on Your Faro Adventure

Consider the insights, memories, and personal development you've earned from your time in this fascinating city as your journey in Faro draws to a conclusion. Here are some questions to get you thinking about your trip to Faro:

1. What were the highlights and most memorable parts of your trip? Was it taking in the local culture, exploring the historic district, or finding hidden gems?

2. Which sights or activities exceeded your expectations and made an impact?

3. Did you have any unusual or unanticipated interactions with locals

that stood out and made your vacation special?

4. How did you interact with the local culture and customs when you were visiting Faro? Did you partake in any regional customs or traditions, go to any cultural events, or try any traditional foods?

5. Consider any instances in which you left your comfort zone to enjoy novel experiences or engage with the neighbourhood.

6. Did you learn more about the culture and way of life of the Algarve through your contacts with locals?

7. **Natural Beauty and Outdoor** Adventures: Which of Faro's natural settings or outdoor pursuits was your favourite? Did you go on any exciting

excursions, take in the breathtaking beaches, or explore the Ria Formosa Natural Park?

8. How did the natural splendour of Faro influence your experience and general well-being?

9. Have you ever had any unplanned encounters with wildlife or peaceful moments in nature that have stayed with you?

10. **Personal Development and Reflection:** Consider the personal effects of your Faro journey. Did you discover something new about yourself, face challenges, or get fresh perspectives?

11. During your stay in Faro, did you have any opportunities for introspection, self-reflection, or personal development?

12. How will your trip's memories and experiences influence your travel plans and view on life going forward?

13. **Connections and Relationships**: Did you interact with people who enhanced your Faro journey, such as residents or other travellers?

14. Think about the connections and relationships you made on your journey. Did any of these interactions change the way you see travel and cross-cultural interactions?

Lessons learned and key takeaways:

- What lessons have you learned most from your trip to Faro? Did you discover something new about yourself, the Algarve, or Portugal?

- How will your future travels and attitude to discovering new places be affected by the experiences and lessons you gained in Faro?

Keep in mind to treasure the moments, document your vacation in Faro with photos and journal entries, and bring the knowledge and lessons learned with you on your upcoming journeys. Without a doubt, Faro has left a lasting impression on your voyage, and the memories from your stay here will continue to motivate and influence your travel adventures in the future.

Printed in Great Britain
by Amazon